The Golden Rule

by

Deborah J. Solberg

Illustrations

by

Joseph G. Bakos

The Golden Rule
2nd Edition 2025

ISBN: **978-1-990442-09-4**

A SUNCITY PRODUCTIONS BOOK FOR CHILDREN
Contemporary fairy-tale with the magic of a spiritual wand.
For more information, visit the website:
DeborahJeanSolberg.com

Once upon a time, Angel fell to the ground.

She only had 1 wing.

"Where is my other wing?"

A heavenly choir sang to her.
"Angel, you will get another wing,
when you do a GOOD DEED"

"A GOOD DEED?? WHAT'S THAT??'
'Maybe, it is peace on earth,
as it is in heaven.
Everyone is nice in heaven,
because they want *to be,*
not because they must *be.*

Angel thought:

'People on earth always want to go to heaven.
It will be easy peasy to do a 'good deed'.

Angel searched for someone who needed a good deed.

She waved as people went by,
    but no one noticed her.
        She was invisible.

        HOW will I get another wing if no one notices me?'

Jester stopped to juggle scarves
    and tell jokes to Baby Dragon.
        But the only one who laughed was Jester.

Then they heard a rapping and a tapping.

Jester stopped laughing and yelled.
"Oh NO! It's Prince.
He said one more bad joke,
and it's off with my head."

Jester grabbed his scarves and ran away.

Prince swung his sword and declared:
"As soon as I learn to sharpen my sword,

it's off with his head.
Then, I'll never have to hear that laugh
or another bad joke again".

He swung his sword again.

Angel ducked but no one noticed Angel.

No, not at all.

She wondered,

"How can I do good deed

and get my second wing,"

Princess ran in with her pet, Baby Dragon.

She tied a pink ribbon around Baby Dragon,
who groaned:

"Pink?
Around my neck?"

Princess said,

"Of course.
Every pet
has a collar around its neck."

"Wait till I get my fire breath,"
grumbled Baby Dragon,
who did not like pink, or collar.

Baby Dragon just wanted to be a .... Dragon.
"And for the record, I am not an 'it.'
I am a 'someone! And I'm someone Special!!"

Baby Dragon stomped off in a huff.

Angel thought,

'Someone Special! Everyone wants to feel Special.'

Angel watched Peasant approach Princess, and said to herself,
*'Peasant must need a good deed
because she is swinging a pail.
This is someone who is Special'.*

Princess interrupted with a scream.

"Ahh! A peasant. Quick ... sanitizer!"

Princess lowered her hand until Peasant bowed lower and lower.

Princess glanced in her mirror and left Peasant on the ground.

Peasant was mad.
"Oh...that makes me so mad, I could just...."

She stomped her foot.
*"Why is it that there is one rule for royalty and
another for the rest of us?
Why do they have so much,
and we have so little?
Why do they get to treat us this way?
There should be one rule for everyone."*

Angel jumped up, and exclaimed,
"One rule for everyone! Oh ... I like that! "

Peasant talked to her pail.
*"That would be worth more than gold!
If I ruled this kingdom,
there would be one Golden Rule."*

Peasant marched back to her village,
swinging her pail in disgust.

Angel pondered.

"AHa! *That's it!*

One Golden Rule. *But wait.*
What IS *the* Golden Rule*?"*

Just then, Wizard followed Jester.

"Jester, telling a joke *is the same as making a cake.*
You need the right ingredients for the job.
And your job is to make people happy."

Jester was puzzled.

> *"But I did that. I said, Knock, knock."*

Wizard shook his head.

> *"Jester...when you told your knock, knock* joke,
> *who actually laughed?"*

Jester laughed,

> *"Me!"*

Wizard sighed.

> *"Only you.*
> *Many people want to laugh but it must be funny.*
> *And not just laugh.*
> *Singing and dancing also make people happy."*

Angel twirled in happiness.

> *"Yes! The* Golden Rule *must make people happy."*

Wizard continued.

> *"And the more people who join in, the better."*

Jester was still puzzled.

> *"Why?"*

The Wizard grabbed him by the hand and twirled around.

"Clap your hands, tap your toes, and twirl around.
How do you feel?,"

Jester joined in.

"Clap your hands, tap your toes, and twirl around.
I feel HAPPY!"

They sang and tapped and twirled.

Jester giggled.

"That was fun.
I don't have to tell a good joke
to make people happy
and that makes me very happy.
You did your good deed for the day, Wizard."

Angel was very excited.

'Good deed for the day! That is it!

1. *One Golden Rule for everyone.*
2. *Everyone joins in, singing and dancing.*
3. *Then they laugh because it is fun, and that makes everyone ...*

Happy!

But what IS the Golden Rule?"

Princess chased Baby Dragon, who had taken off her pink ribbon.

Baby Dragon yelped.

"No!! I won't wear a pink ribbon."

Princess tied Baby Dragon's ribbon back around her neck.   Again!

Prince and Princess squabbled. Should the ribbon be *pink* or *blue*.

Prince whined,

> "I don't know why Mumsie is making us go to this festival."

> 'With peasants!"

Sneered the Princess.

> "It is all your fault."

They squabbled again about whose fault it was.

Baby Dragon roared a tiny roar.

Prince and Princess stopped squabbling.

> "What was that?"

asked Prince.

Baby Dragon replied with great dignity.

> "My roar."

Prince and Princess roared with laughter.

> "Is that the best you can do?"

Baby Dragon was offended.

*"I am still just a baby dragon,
and your fighting is hurting my ears."*

Peasant ran to them, waving her pail in distress.
*"The village well is broken.
The people have no clean water."*

Princess said,

"Oh, dear. That's too bad."

Prince sighed,

*" Well, we have no water to spare.
We could give you gold,
but there is no water to buy so we won't."*

Peasant pleaded.

"Please help us fix the well."

Princess scoffed.

"Fix? You mean, like work??"

Prince and Princess both laughed again.

Peasant was quite stern.

> *"But if we do not have water to grow your food,
> you will starve, and the kingdom will die."*

Prince and Princess looked at each other in shock,
and then, squabbled about food.

Baby Dragon roared.   Just a little bit LOUDER!

The squabbling stopped.

Shaking her head, Peasant asked,
"Who's in charge?"

Prince shrugged.
"Good question.
Mumsie and Dada have gone to the royalty conference."
"You could try Uncle Wizard."
"He is probably at the Magic Academy
making nasty spells."

Peasant rolled her eyes.
"Everyone passes the buck.
Fine, I will look for Uncle Wizard."

Prince watched her go.
"I wish I was brave like that.
But saving anything
would mean doing something."

Princess was curious.
"What is stopping you?"

Prince thought about it for just a second or two.
"I am not a real knight, yet.
I haven't learned how to sharpen my sword."

Baby Dragon jumped into the conversation.
"So, when do I get to fly and breathe fire?"

Princess wagged her finger and looked in her mirror.
"Not until you are older."

Baby Dragon bounced with excitement.
"I can hardly wait to be a real fire-breathing dragon.
Then, I will save the world."

Prince swished his sword in the air.
"Take your time.
When you start breathing fire in the village,
I must slay you.
It's in my job description."

Baby Dragon frowned.
"Iieeeuu.
I don't want to breathe fire in the village."

Princess skipped off, saying,
"No one is slaying anyone.
Mumsie will not let you."

Meanwhile, Angel was in despair.
"Hello, out there.
I'm an angel from heaven,
giving away one good deed
free of charge.
Any takers?"

Peasant rushed to her, swinging the pail overhead.
"Me!"

Angel breathed a sigh of relief!

"You heard me!"

Peasant begged.

*"Please help my village.
Our well is broken.*

Angel's one wing drooped.

"I didn't say I could fix a well."

"What kind of good deed is that?"

frowned Peasant.

Angel shrugged.

*"Beggars can't be choosers, you know.
And you are a …. "*

"A peasant."

sighed Peasant.

*"I think I know that.
But if you are a real angel,
where is your other wing?"*

Angel fluffed up her one wing.
"Uh.... wings are just a technicality."
Look, I must do an official good deed for someone and
THEN I get my other wing."

Peasant stomped off, grumbling as she went.
"What good is a good deed if I can't use it?
My village needs help, not me."

Angel sank down on a tree stump, stumped as to what to do next.

Along came Jester, who sat down beside her, just as stumped.

Then Baby Dragon sat down beside them, also, quite stumped.

Their heads turned to a sound.

A tapping and a rapping that sounded very much like ....

"Prince!"
yelped Jester, who hid behind the rock.

Sure enough, Prince danced in, tapping his sword on his shoes.

Baby Dragon muttered,

> *"I don't think he is doing that sword thing right."*

Jester whispered, loudly,

> *"Which is probably a good thing in your case.
> Princes are knights who slay dragons, y' know."*

Baby Dragon chuckled.

> *"The only thing he's going to slay is his toe."*

Angel nodded.

> *"But dancing is better than slaying."*

No one heard Angel.

No, not at all.

Angel wondered why no one could hear her but Peasant.

Jester jumped up.

> *"Hah! He's a coward.
> Frightened of his own shadow. Watch this."*

Jester called out to Prince,

"It is I, me, the Jester, Your Royal Highness,
with another bad, terrible, rotten, no-good
knock knock joke!
So, bring it on, sword man."

Prince hesitated.

Jester said to Baby Dragon.

"There, what did I tell you?
Prince is a coward."

and left, laughing as he went.

Prince yelled after him,

"I am not a coward!"

There was just silence. Not even one little ha ha.

Prince sat down beside Baby Dragon.

"I am, too."

"Really? You are a coward?"
exclaimed Baby Dragon.

Prince nodded.

"I have no courage to use my sword. "

He whispered.

"Don't tell anyone, but I don't like red*."*

Angel and Baby Dragon echoed,

Red? Red what?"

Prince sighed.

He waived his sword, making a rapping sound on his shoes.
"I just want to make music."

Baby Dragon said,
"Tut, tut. We must learn our jobs.
I breathe fire.
You, sword fight ...
like this."

Grabbing the sword, Baby Dragon, poked, stabbed,
circled, and lunged in the air.

Prince shook his head, and sighed, again.

Baby Dragon handed him the sword,
took off the pink ribbon
and waved it at Prince.

"Chase me.
After you practice the moves,
then you won't be afraid anymore."

Prince grinned, and off they went on a great chase.

Angel watched them jumping, dodging, hiding,
and having a lot of fun.

Prince chased Baby Dragon, until his arm went up in the air
with the sword –
high over Baby Dragon's head.

Baby Dragon looked up at the sword.
"Are you going to slay me now"?

Prince's arm froze. He could not move it. No, not at all.
"I cannot do it."

His arm lowered.   His sword clattered to the ground.

Prince sank on the rock, very sad.
"I'm not going to be a very good Prince."

Baby Dragon was relieved.
"Did you stop because you are afraid?"

Prince shook his head.
*"I am not afraid anymore,
but I'd rather have fun, than fight.
A real prince doesn't slay a friend."*

Baby Dragon was so happy to be Prince's friend.
Wanna play again?"

Prince nodded with a grin.

He jumped up and grabbed his sword to chase Baby Dragon.

Princess stopped them.
"Baby Dragon, there you are.
I have been looking everywhere for you.
Mommy is very, very lonesome.
Where is your pink *ribbon?"*

Baby Dragon jumped up and down.
"I took it off.
Pink *is not my signature color,*
and I am not wearing a collar for anyone.
Come and get me, Prince."

And off they ran.

Princess shouted after them,
"Come and get me, Prince?
Some pet you are, Baby Dragon."

"I need a friend right now. *Peasant!*"
Princess bellowed.

Princess snapped her fingers.

Peasant came running, still waving her pail.

When Peasant saw Princess, she stopped.

Princess looked up from her mirror and demanded.
"Come here and be my friend."

Peasant crossed her arms and tapped her toe.

Princess put her hands on her hips, getting impatient.
"I'm waiting!"

Peasant scoffed.
"You cannot make me be your friend if I don't want to."

Princess was shocked.
"You can't talk that way to a Princess."

Peasant said,

*"And the way you talk to me
is why you don't have any friends.
Real friends are friends
because they want to be.
When you snap your fingers,
you think you are better than me,
and then I'm a servant,
not your friend.
And I refuse to be your servant, anymore!"*

Peasant snapped her fingers back at Princess.

Princess sank down and grabbed Peasant by the ankle.

Princess begged,

"Wait. I'm sorry. I didn't realize that I was being so, so...."

Peasant humphed.

"Nasty?"

Princess nodded.

"And selfish?"

Princess nodded.

"And obnoxious?"

Peasant humphed again.

Princess hesitated and whined.
"That's a little harsh,"

Peasant pulled away.

*"No, no, wait.
I really do want you to be my friend.
I always did.
I just didn't think princesses and peasants
could be friends.
But I want us to be friends.
Now.
I mean,
please."*

Peasant looked doubtful.
*"Why would I want to?
You haven't been nice to me at all."*

Princess pondered that thought.
"I will fix your well??"

Peasant looked more doubtful.
"You? You will fix my well?"

Princess pondered that thought even more.

"Well, I might have to order someone to do it,
but I am good at that,
so, it will be done.
I promise!"

Peasant hemmed and hawed.

"Wellllll...."

Princess rushed on,

> *"My name is Sally.*
> *I know.*
> *It is a bad Princess name.*

Peasant replied,

> *"I am Charlotte."*

Princess smiled a real smile.

> *"Charlotte is such a princess name.*
> *Sally is so...Sally.*
> *C'mon. Let's go fix*
> *A hole*
> *in the bottom of the well."*

Peasant sang with her."

> *There's a hole*
> *in the bottom of the well."*

They both sang together.

> *"There's a hole,*
> *there's a hole,*
> *there's a hole*
> *in the bottom of the well."*

They danced off to fix ...

       the hole in the bottom of the well.

Angel waved at Peasant, but Peasant did not see Angel anymore.

Angel was sad.

       'I am doomed to be a one-winged Angel.
       Useless. Nobody will want me in heaven now.'

Jester sauntered in, juggling his scarves,
       and humming to himself.

Wizard crept up behind him and pounced.
       "Aren't you supposed to be at the Magic Academy, Jester?"

Jester moaned.
                "Oh, Wizard.
       I am never going to be a good Jester.
       I could study at the Magic Academy forever,
       and I will never make anyone laugh,
                but me."

Wizard's wand zipped in the air.
                "Find your passion,
       something you love to do so much,
       that it's as important as breathing air."

Jester twisted his scarves.
       "Can't I be happy without passion?"

Angel couldn't sit still any longer.

She yelled, thinking no one would hear her.
                "Oh, for heaven's sake.
       Everyone *has passion."*

Jester and Wizard startled, looking for the new voice.

They both called out.

"Who is that?"

Angel jumped up on the rock with great excitement.
"Did you hear me?"

"I heard that",

said Wizard.

"Come out where we can see you."

Angel waved at them.
"Over here. In white. Half wing. Can't miss me."

She flew down from the rock and crashed into them.
"Ouch!"

She sat up, breathless.

Wizard tsked tsked.
*"You are not very good at what you do, either.
But we don't give angel lessons at the Magic Academy.
We can't help you."*

Angel ticked off on her fingers.
*"You have helped me already.
You said that everyone needs the Golden Rule.
There must be one rule for everyone.
It must be fun.
And the more people who join in, the more powerful it is.
But I do not know what the rule is.
And I need to know!"*

Wizard waved his wand.

"Oh, that Golden Rule *is the oldest rule on the books,
but no one ever pays attention to it anymore."*

Jester and Angel were puzzled.
"What IS it?"

Wizard was curious.
"You really want to know?"

Jester and Angel nodded.

*"You must be ready to know it,
or it will do no good.
Are you really ready?"*

"YES!"
They said, *very loudly.*

Wizard wrote the words in the air with his and.
"Treat others as you want to be treated."

Angel and Jester danced around Wizard, echoing,
"Treat others as you want to be treated."

Angel stopped and said,
"Why don't people pay attention to it."

Wizard tapped his head with his wand.
"Because it's hard to always think nice thoughts
and do nice things, even when no one is looking.
Especially, when they get nothing in return.
That's why most people don't see Angels."

Angel was ecstatic.
"Perfect! Now, I know the Golden Rule!"

Wizard tapped Angel on her wingless shoulder.
"Knowing the Golden Rule
does not get you another wing.
Even I cannot make a spell that powerful."
"Words without action are just words.
Words with action make things change."

Just then, Prince danced in,
tapping a rapping beat with his sword on his heels.
It was a happy dance.

Dancing their own beat right behind him
were Princess and Peasant and Baby Dragon.

"We fixed the hole in the bottom of the well!"
They sang with such joy, Angel thought they sounded
like a heavenly choir on earth.

Jester joined in with his scarves, so happy
that he did not have to be funny.

zard starting toe tapping and wand-waving to his own beat!
"This is it, Angel
...the magic of the Golden Rule!

It's not the words but what you do with the words.

'Treat others as you want to be treated.'
And... it only takes one person to pass it on.
When everyone joins in, then everyone is truly happy."

Angel twirled around them, singing her own song.
"That's my good deed.
I can fly now.
I'll go everywhere.
I'll tell everyone.
The Golden Rule is my good deed every day.
Soon, the whole world will live the Golden Rule!
Then every Angel will have both wings, just like me!"

Jester pointed at Angel's shoulder,

> *"Look, there is a golden wing.*
> *Now, that is a song to sing!*
> *Long Live the Golden Rule!"*

They all joined in.

Their happiness made Angel's wing grow and grow,
until she could lift off the ground.

And so, the story went.

    The Kingdom began to live the Golden Rule.

Every day, the people found ways to do good deeds and
    make happiness grow.

Angel flew around the world to spread the word,
    and soon, the whole world lived, 'Happily Ever After.'

The End …. is only the Beginning.

About the Author

Deborah Jean Solberg

Is founding Artistic Director of Theatrix Youtheatre Society located in British Columbia, Canada. Theatrix was incorporated as a non-profit charitable performing arts organization for children in 1991. Over the last three decades, she collaborated with thousands of children to create shows as a vehicle to learn confidence and self-expression.

Deborah produced and directed over 100 productions, from short school touring shows to full scale musical theatre productions and is a 17-time Theatre BC festival award winner.

Deborah is playwright of over 30 original plays, with a passion for adapting classical children's literature.   Deborah's own children's stories have a strong spiritual context to help shape the character of children into kind and compassionate human beings. Each story has been inspired by real people or real events.

Deborah has not only had the pleasure of watching several alumni become professional actors, dancers. and singers around the world but is proud of the many friendships that have endured over time.

She hopes her readership enjoys her take on the contemporary fairy tale.

About the Illustrator

Joseph G. Bakos

Joseph worked for Varga Cartoon Studios, which worked on Rugrats,
Mr. Bean Cartoons, Real Monsters, etc.

He has also worked in game developing for more than 10 years.
at Invictus Games Ltd.

Joseph continues to work freelance on
children's books, comics, web design and other illustrations.

Other Children's Books in the
Empowerment Stories Series
by
Deborah Jean Solberg

The Happy Mirror
Rain Dancer
My Favorite
Super Cape
Little Star

Check out DeborahJeanSolberg.com
https://www.facebook.com/deborahjeansolberg

(Please report any book quality issues.)